GRANNY SCARECROW

Books by Anne Stevenson

POETRY

Living in America (Generation Press,
  University of Michigan, USA, 1965)
Reversals (Wesleyan University Press, USA, 1969)
Travelling Behind Glass: Selected Poems 1963-1973
  (Oxford University Press, 1974)
Correspondences, a Family History in Letters
  (Oxford University Press, 1974)
Enough of Green (Oxford University Press, 1977)
Sonnets for Five Seasons (Five Seasons Press, 1979)
Minute by Glass Minute (Oxford University Press, 1982)
A Legacy (Taxvs Press, 1983)
The Fiction Makers (Oxford University Press, 1985)
Wintertime (MidNAG, 1986)
Selected Poems 1956-1986 (Oxford University Press, 1987)
The Other House (Oxford University Press, 1990)
Four and a Half Dancing Men (Oxford University Press, 1993)
The Collected Poems 1955-1995
  (Oxford University Press, 1996; Bloodaxe Books, 2000)
Granny Scarecrow (Bloodaxe Books, 2000)

LITERARY CRITICISM & BIOGRAPHY

Elizabeth Bishop (Twayne, USA, 1966)
Bitter Fame: A Life of Sylvia Plath
  (Viking, 1989; Houghton Mifflin, USA, 1989)
Between the Iceberg and the Ship: Selected Essays
  (University of Michigan Press, 1998)
Five Looks at Elizabeth Bishop
  (Bellew/Agenda Editions, 1998)

ANNE STEVENSON

Granny Scarecrow

BLOODAXE BOOKS

Copyright © Anne Stevenson 2000

ISBN: 1 85224 534 4

First published 2000 by
Bloodaxe Books Ltd,
P.O. Box 1SN,
Newcastle upon Tyne NE99 1SN.

Bloodaxe Books Ltd acknowledges
the financial assistance of Northern Arts.

Cover printing by J. Thomson Colour Printers Ltd, Glasgow.

Printed in Great Britain by
Cromwell Press Ltd, Trowbridge, Wiltshire.

For Nerys Johnson

whose spirit is a durable fire

Acknowledgements

Acknowledgements are due to the editors of the following publications where some of these poems or earlier versions of them first appeared: *Critical Quarterly, Dark Horse, The Hudson Review, Last Words* (Picador, 1999), *The Michigan Quarterly Review, Planet, PN Review, Poetry Wales, Tabla* and *Thumbscrew*. 'A Ballad for Apothecaries' was commissioned by the Salisbury Festival for the Last Words project (1999) for display in a chemists' shop. 'Burning the News' was commissioned by David Hart and Rogan Wolf for their *waiting room poems* project (2000). 'On Going Deaf' first appeared as a broadside (poster-poem) published by Aralia Press, West Chester University, Pennsylvania.

Five poems – 'Incident', 'Suicide', 'Skills', 'Poem for Harry Fainlight' and 'To Witness Pain Is a Different Form of Pain' – were published in earlier collections by Oxford University Press. Four have been revised and I now think of them as finished. The last I consider to be so appropriate as a tribute to this book's dedicatee that I couldn't leave it out.

Contents

III

I

Vertigo

Mind led body
to the edge of the precipice.
They stared in desire
at the naked abyss.
If you love me, said mind,
take that step into silence.
If you love me, said body,
turn and exist.

Innocence and Experience

I laid myself down as a woman
And woke as a child.
Sleep buried me up to my chin,
But my brain cut wild.

Sudden summer lay sticky as tar
Under bare white feet.
Stale, soot-spotted heapings of winter
Shrank in the street.

Black headlines, infolded like napkins,
Crashed like grenades
As war beat its way porch by porch
Up New Haven's façades.

Europe: a brown hive of noises,
Hitler inside.
On the too sunny shelf by the stairs
My tadpoles died.

Big boys had already decided
Who'd lose and who'd score,
Singing one potato, two potato,
Three potato, four.

Singing sticks and stones
May break my bones
(but names hurt more).

Singing step on a crack
Break your mother's back
(her platinum-ringed finger).

Singing who got up your mother
When your daddy wasn't there?
Singing allee allee in free! You're
Dead, you're dead, wherever you are!

The White Room

Long summer shadows calm the grass,
each figure a finger.
Which ones are pointing to the past,
which to the future?

The tiny grey grandmother
loosens an immense shadow.
We shiver in it, but for her
it's a pontoon to the handsome fellow

she married – when was it
they honeymooned in the Philippines?
Teddy Roosevelt was President,
and he'd sent the marines

to educate the Filipinos; God
advancing with his stick.
And grandfather was Christian-good,
but he came home sick,

and the baby died; then money troubles,
syphilis and silence as he sank
into the brass-locked, tissue-papered culls
of her steamer trunk.

How it hunches there, anchored hulk
in the surf of her candlewick bedcover
in the bride-white room we had to visit
with its incense of Bible-leather,
mothballs and sweet unappeasable hurt.

A Surprise on the First Day of School
(1938)

They give you a desk with a lid, mother.
They let you keep your book.
My desk's next to the window.
I can see the trees.
But you mustn't look out the window
    at light on the leaves.
You must look at the book.

A nice-smelling, shiny book, mother,
With words in it and pictures.
I mostly like the pictures,
    some of them animals and birds.
But you mustn't look at the pictures.
You don't *ever* read the pictures.
You read the words!

Going Back
(Ann Arbor, October 1993)

It hazes over,
blurred by forty years,
a nerveless place,
like the idea of pain,
like love affairs
that at the time *were* time.

An intimate alias,
half mine,
floats on these streets,
identifies each elm
that isn't there,
breathes in these
shapeless, lax,
companionable homes,
hand-built midwest America
that clones itself
in leafy, bypassed towns
steepled, asleep on
ochre-coloured lawns,
named for the dead that still
fadingly mark a street, a school,
its sledding hill and park.

And next? When I next come?
More will be gone.
The underwater palimpsest
may be all but illegible,
may even release me
from haunted erasures,
more haunting survivals –
Mrs Winter's
witch's den of cures
now flaunts a showy extension
with red doors.
How strong, in spite of that,
its tell-tale reek of compost,
eau de chat.

Behind a veil of murky conifers,
screened by her purple-brown veranda,
Miss Elizabeth Dean, at ninety-four
(a hundred and thirty-four?)
entices, still, with an *epergne*
of ripple-ribboned candies
young neighbours she'll outlive;
as she outlived the elms
(those smoky autumns
drugged with burning leaves)
as she at last outlived
all her contemporaries.

She willed her virgin wealth
to the city's trees. And who,
among our PhDs and kindly
Democratic wives would
forty years ago have guessed that,
thanks to old Miss Dean,
while maples last,
Ann Arbor will remain an
arbour, releasing from October's
gentle hospice leaves like hands
that beg to go, let go,
let go, regretfully, a salmon one,
a crimson one, a yellow one,
brimming the sidewalks and shallow gutters
with yet another generation,
another kickable pile.

A mobile municipal vacuum-leafer
roars with gluttony outside
the Newcombs' house,
its chocolate porch no longer
painted chocolate;
now by the Bursley's grander brick,
no longer Mr & Mrs Bursley's.
At sixteen, waking on our sleeping porch,
I wrote a sonnet to the morning
'walking like a dancer'
on Miss Dean's shimmering, weedless,
surely eternal front lawn.

Our house wants paint.
The porches have been glassed in.
With the side fence gone,
how shrunken the little summer house.
New owners shut their white blinds
tight as eyelids, but I see through
to that famous 'L',
living-room bought for two
pianos to live in.
It brought up two girls – three –
too carefully, too musically.

Is it a brace or a fetter,
never to be set quite free
from vanished elms we took for granted,
angel-food cake and mother's
League of Women Voters,
mother and faithful Mother Destler,
Mrs Florer, deaf, next door,
and further down, remote as Greek,
foundering in sadness I crossed
to get away from, Mister Blake?

John Keats, 1821–1950

Keats was Miss McKinney's class, 12th grade English,
and we could tell she loved him
by the way she scolded us. 'Why is it
you young, spoiled people never look?'

Poetry was what we learned 'by heart'.
I can still see it, that clammy, Coke-stained textbook's
Ode to Autumn. I think I half believed I was him,
the spirit of Keats come back, in me, to Michigan.

Devoid of thatch-eaves, lambs and granary floors,
Ann Arbor had its river. I hymned the sallows under
violent-coloured maples. Crickets I remember,
and how the fierce gnats' wailing was oracular.

Arioso Dolente

(for my grandchildren when they become grandparents)

Mother, who read and thought and poured herself into me;
she was the jug and I was the two-eared cup.
How she would scorn today's 'show-biz inanity,
democracy twisted, its high ideals sold up!'
       Cancer filched her voice, then cut her throat.
           Why is it
      none of the faces in this family snapshot
          looks upset?

Father, who ran downstairs as I practised the piano;
barefooted, buttoning his shirt, he shouted 'G,
D-natural, C-*flat*! *Dolente, arioso.*
Put all the griefs of the world in that change of key.'
       Who then could lay a finger on his sleeve
          to distress him with
    'One day, Steve, two of your well-taught daughters
          will be deaf.'

Mother must be sitting, left, on the porch-set,
you can just see her. My sister's on her lap.
And that's Steve confiding to his cigarette
something my mother's mother has to laugh at.
       The screened door twangs, slamming
          on its sprung hinge.
    Paint blisters on the steps; iced tea, grasscuttings,
         elm flowers, mock orange...

A grand June evening, like this one, not too buggy,
unselfquestioning midwestern, maybe 1951.
And, of course, there in my grandmother's memory
lives just such another summer – 1890 or 91.
       Though it's not on her mind now/then.
          No, she's thinking of
    the yeast-ring rising in the oven. Or how *any* shoes
         irritate her bunion.

Paper gestures, pictures, newsprint laughter.
And after the camera winks and makes its catch,
the decibels drain away *for ever and ever.*
No need to say 'Look!' to these smilers on the porch,
       'Grandmother will have her stroke,
          and you, mother, will nurse her.'
Or to myself, this woman died paralysed-dumb, and that one
          dumb from cancer.

Sufficient unto the day... Grandmother, poor and liturgical,
whose days were duties, stitches in the tea-brown blanket
she for years crocheted, its zigzag of yellow wool,
her grateful offering, her proof of goodness to present,
       gift-wrapped, to Our Father in Heaven. 'Accept,
         O Lord, this best-I-can-make-it soul.'
And He: 'Thou good and faithful sevant, lose thyself
         and be whole.'

Consciousness walks on tiptoe through what happens.
So much is felt, so little of it said.
But ours is the breath on which the past depends.
'What happened' is what the living teach the dead,
       who, smilingly lost to their lost concerns,
         in grey on grey,
       are all of them deaf, blind, unburdened
         by today.

As if our recording selves, our mortal identities,
could be cupped in a concave universe or lens,
ageless at all ages, cleansed of memories,
not minding that meaningful genealogy extends
       no further than mind's flash images reach back.
         As for what happens next,
         let all the griefs of the world
         find keys for that.

Arioso dolente: from Beethoven's piano sonata, opus 110,
third movement; introduction to the fugue.

'Love Stories and a Bed of Sand'
(after a photograph of graffiti by Jamie Ross)

In flood, familiar footpaths and
childhood cycle ways, heel-trodden mud
packed firm between arthritic roots;
anglers, picnickers, comforting as woodcuts.
The way things used to be,
should be, should have been?
Sensibility is a strange sandbag.
The picture book
lies down in level water as I look.

Persons, those personal *I*s.
Suppose they're crying from their *e*s and *o*s.
No one. No one.
Here's a stone with a severed name.
Anyone at home?
Did DP or VB spraypaint that heart?
Who crept in alone to smear it out?
Mind whispers, *sadist, masochist, rapist.*
Rust-stains on a blanched wall only exist.

Hold your hand over a flashlight
or up to strong sunlight,
and there's your blood and you
red as coals perishing.
A piece of star that feels, a meteor that sees,
loves, labels as it looks.
But what's that furnace in those drowning books?
By flood, by fire, by straining human hand,
love stories and a bed of sand.

II

Moonrise

While my anxiety stood phoning you last evening,
My simpler self lay marvelling through glass
At the full moon marbling the clouds, climbing
In shafts, a headlamp through an underpass,
Until it swung free, cratered, deadly clear,
Earth's stillborn twin unsoiled by life or air.

And while our voices huddled mouth to ear,
I watched tenacity of long imagination
Cast her again in a film of the old goddess,
Chaste of the chase, more virgin than the Virgin,
Lifting herself from that rucked, unfeeling waste
As from the desert of her own ruined face.

Such an unhinging light. To see her. To see that.
As no one else had seen her. Or might see that.

Clydie is dead!

Our lar, our little mammal.
Though his last day didn't believe it.
It kept on moving at its usual heartless pace
over and around a hollow cat-space.

We buried him by the toolshed.
The cat flap wouldn't believe it,
so we sealed its chattering mouth.
We seized and scrubbed his feeding bowls
and sent them to a far shelf.

The fact is, nothing in the house could bear it
when Clyde dropped out of himself...
who waxed loquacious on the subject of roast meat
and cat's rights, who took favours
from my fingers at mealtimes as just deserts,
who always kept his dress-shirt spinnaker-white
while extending an urgent tongue to his tabby parts;
who reserved for himself, every morning,
a place on a lap, whereon for a while he might
subdue a human; upon whose face
the cat-painter's brush had slipped a little
applying the Chinese white; for which he received
in compensation, huge Indonesian eyes –
polished jet in a setting of crinkled topaz;

whose tail was so long he could wrap himself up in it;

who could fill with his length, without exertion,
the entire shelf over the radiator;
who was adept at the art of excretion,
and discreet as to the burying of personal treasure.

Dear, wise Clyde, who after tyrannical Bonnie died,
thrived in her absence, Hadrian after Domitian,
you will never again rule us by vocative law,
or pull back the bedclothes at six with a firm paw,
or bemoan the indignities of travelling by car,
or flourish an upright tail on crepuscular walks,
no, nor compile statistics on the field mice of Wales.

Pwllymarch was your chief estate,
you whom Oxford made and Cambridge unmade,
though Hay-on-Wye and Durham made you great.
Much travelled, valuable, voluble Clyde,
who said so much, yet never spoke a word,
                requiescat.

Incident

She must have been about
twelve in 1942.

She stood in front
of the tall hall mirror
and she made a mou.
With her pretty not-
yet-kissed mouth she made an ugly
mou mou
that didn't mean anything
she knew.
So bony, so skinny,
and so very naked.
Little pink belled swellings.
Two.

The mirror did what she did.
Mou mou. Mou mou.

Nowhere to go.
Nothing to do.

Suicide

There was no hole in the universe to fit him.
He felt it as he fooled around. No rim,
no closet, nowhere to hide. The moon
also was fooling. He told
the girl and she giggled. 'As much for you
as for anyone.' But it wasn't true.

Spiders with their eight eyes, snails had more to do.

'When I said I wouldn't kiss him
he said he'd slash his wrists.
He was always saying stupid things like this.'

He saw himself entering women.
Wide open hay-scented barn, transistor on,
heavy rhythm of drums to draw him in.
And then that smallness, tiny loop at the end
where a slipknot tightened over light until a fist
struck. Darkness swelled around him like a breast.

The noose? A way of playing let's pretend.
A dare, a joke, the freedom of the risk.
He was free as air when the girl's father found him,
returning from an evening out with friends.

Skills

Like threading a needle by computer, to align
the huge metal-plated tracks of the macadam-spreader
with two frail ramps to the plant-carrier.
Working alone on Sunday, overtime,
the driver powers the wheel: forward, reverse, forward
centimetre by centimetre… stop!

He leaps from the cab, a carefree Humphrey Bogart,
to check both sides. The digger sits up front
facing backwards at an angle to the flat,
its diplodocus-neck chained to a steel scaffold.
Its head fits neatly in the macadam-spreader's lap.
Satisfying. All of a piece and tightly wrapped.

Before he slams himself, whistling, into his load,
he eyes all six, twelve, eighteen, twenty-four tyres.
Imagine a plane ascending. Down on the road,
this clever Matchbox toy that takes apart
grows small, now smaller still and more compact,
a crawling speck on the unfolding map.

An Angel

After a long drive west into Wales,
as I lay on my bed, waiting
for my mind to seep back through my body,
I watched two gothic panels draw apart.
Between them loomed an angel,
tall as a caryatid, wingless,
draped like Michelangelo's sibyl.
Never have I felt so profoundly looked into.

She was bracing on her hip an immense book
that at first I took for a Bible. Then
prickling consciousness seemed to apprehend
The Recording Angel.
The pen she wielded writhed like a caduceus,
and on the book
ECCE LIBER MORI had been branded.

This book she held out towards me,
arm-muscles tensing, but even as I reached
I knew it was too heavy to hold.
Its gravity, she made me feel, would crush me,
a black hole of infinitely compressed time.
Each page weighed as much as the world.

Drawing my attention to a flaw in the book's crust –
a glazed porthole, a lens of alizarin –
she focused it (it must have been a microscope)
and silently motioned me to look.
Fire folding fire was all I saw. Then the red glass
cleared and a blizzard of swimming cells
swept underneath it, lashing their whip-like tails,
clashing, fusing, consuming each other greedily,
fountaining into polyps and underwater flowers.
Soon – fast-forward – forests were shooting up.
Seasons tamed lagoons of bubbling mud
where, hatching from the scum, animalculae
crawled, swarmed, multiplied, disbanded,
swarmed again, raised cities out of dust,
destroyed them, died. I turned to the angel,

'Save these species,' I cried.
And brought my face right down on her book,
my cheek on the lens like a lid.

Instantly I knew I had put out a light
that had never been generated by a book.
That vision-furnace, that blink into genesis?
Nothing but a passing reflection of the angel.

Rising, for the first time afraid,
I confronted her immortality
circling like a bracelet of phosphorus
just outside the windscreen of the car.
For it seems I was still driving.
Solidity and substance disappeared.
A noose of frenzied, shimmering electrons,
motes of an approaching migraine,
closed around me.
And through that fluorescent manacle,
the road flowed on through Wales.

Granny Scarecrow

Tears flowed at the chapel funeral,
more beside the grave on the hill. Nevertheless,
after the last autumn ploughing,
they crucified her old flowered print housedress
live, on a pole.

Marjorie and Emily, shortcutting to school,
used to pass and wave; mostly Gran would wave back.
Two white Sunday gloves
flapped good luck from the crossbar; her head's plastic sack
would nod, as a rule.

But when winter arrived, her ghost thinned.
The dress began to look starved in its field of snowcorn.
One glove blew off and was lost.
The other hung blotchy with mould from the hedgerow, torn
by the wind.

Emily and Marjorie noticed this.
Without saying why, they started to avoid the country way
through the cornfield. Instead they walked
from the farm up the road to the stop where they
caught the bus.

And it caught them. So in time they married.
Marjorie, divorced, rose high in the catering profession.
Emily had children and grandchildren, though,
with the farm sold, none found a cross to fit their clothes when
Emily and Marjorie died.

Freeing Lizzie

(i.m. Elizabeth Jane Jones, 1905-1999)

Don't mistake it for a camera snapping day.
Instamatics ought to flash for a family occasion,
but today photography has stayed away;
nothing here for display case or mantelpiece,
though the chapel's packed. Exposed in her high place
in front of the stained brown rail around the pulpit,
the elderly organist struggles to pacify her face.
Like everyone else, she's in black,
and the tremulous hymns she plays – the same strains
over and over – loop themselves around the yellowing
plaster and pale windows like black bunting.
Lizzie, had she been with us, would have worn a hat.
Among the last of a hat-wearing generation,
she would have sat in front, upright, eagerly proper.
What will young Reverend Jones have to say about her?

The organ pauses, recommences; everyone rises.
Like spontaneous applause, the first sung hymn
thunders from the pews, peal after peal of Welsh voices.
Self-conscious in ties and suits, Iddon, Gwynfor,
Hefin, Meirion, Aled, Alun bear the coffin,
bumping it gently through the chapel door,
down the side aisle to a raised bier by the platform.
Three ministers, one handsome with silver hair, close in.
They offer a kindly confident, protective power.
Except for a spray of pink roses, the box is bare.
Can it be Lizzie who is shut in there?

Failing to make himself small, the largest grandson stands
cramped by the wall next to a less lofty cousin.
They can't think what to do with their hands.
We who don't speak Welsh, who listen with our eyes
and can't think what to do with our tears,
take comfort. Right words are being said in the right way.
It could be these family faces, these rows of afterlives,
are meeting and merging somewhere with a crowd of others.
Would Lizzie's strong-handed forebears have stayed away?
Parents, grandparents, great aunties in pre-war frocks
must be pouring out of the bronze age seams of the valley,
hastening to help Lizzie out of that box!

There was a song Lizzie liked about a ruined girl
who drowned herself for love in her father's well.
An unmarried aunt at Nant Pasgan used to sing it,
milking the cows at evening, and Lizzie could hear it still –
'a very sad song' – floating out from the ruins of the barn
when we drove her 'home'. It was her only visit.
And that was all the sadness we had from Lizzie.
Beautiful, drownable girls have ballads to live in.
Plain ones can't be picky. They have to marry who comes.
Yet, in God's hands, a marriage's ups and downs
can be the wellspring under the rock that founts a river.
So it was, at least, with Lizzie, who when her brother died
– their hope, their heir, the most beloved one –
gave up her only son (it was a Bible family) to the farm.
'Llawer o ferched, dim mab, a heb etifedd i gadw'r tir.'
The pain of it! But then she had daughters
who married and had sons and daughters, and those
daughters' daughters have sons, and so now, so then...

A pause. A prayer introduces the last hymn,
then the blessing. We shuffle out, heads, eyes down,
which may be why no living soul sees Lizzie,
up and among us, free, smiling at everyone.
Look, look, she's everywhere! Relief leaves us blinking,
chaffing, thanking Reverend Jones, *'gwasanaeth hyfryd,'*
deciding which relatives will ride with whom.
For the ceremony of the cemetery is to come;
Lizzie's bones have to be tucked in with other bones.
Meanwhile, Lizzie's gone ahead to the Cadwgan.
It's going to be a treat of a tea: salmon, beef, cucumber sandwiches,
sausages on frilly sticks, canapés, satays, vol-au-vents,
five kinds of cake besides the bara brith and fruit scones,
yes, and an eighteenth – or twentieth? – great-grandson
who will have to be shown off, chuckled over, noisily passed around.

Llawer o ferched...: 'Many daughters, no son, without an heir to keep the land.'
gwasanaeth hyfryd: a good service

Morning Exercise

(Pwllymarch, Gwynedd, July 1997)

Like? Like what, that rare morning mist
peeling off the *morfa*?

Like unshorn ewe's fleece in July
unbandaging in soiled, rheum-coloured hanks.
Newborn wool, rose-white rose-pink, shimmers beneath.

Like smoke out of Apollyon's mandibles,
as footsore Christian, easing free his burden,
hurls it from a brightening threshold. Ah, salvation!

Like history, raped Europa's incubus.
Forked by the sun, turned
by long tines of light into a light harvest.

Let's take breakfast out to the terrace
and deliquesce into summer forgetfulness.

Behind the barn, fog-feathered grass
scatters a sopping largess.
Is that a line of sheep? No, marsh meadowsweet
slipping a vein of cloud over iron brown peat.

A *morfa* in Welsh refers to a fen or sea-marsh,
usually found at the foot of mountains.

Phoenicurus phoenicurus

Phu-eet! Phu-eet! Mr unresting redstart has something to be
anxious about. A nest of eggs? Babies? Or has he
lost them already to the weasel, scared away yesterday,

slithering (guilty? sinister?) out of a rock hole?
Phu-eet, on and on, a tiny, uptilted, not really hysterical
shriek. Greeting his mate on top of the clothes pole…

gone. Divers? No, rust-tinted streamers, each, so to speak,
with an end of invisible raffia in its beak.
So where is the camouflaged nook or lichenous crack

that has to be wicker-worked, netted inside those flights?
Such showy displays and flash, panic-coloured lights.
Calm down, pretty bird! You've been gulping big bites

from my reading and writing all morning. Stay still!
What wars do you have to survive, with your phoenix tail
in all that Darwinian weather, too small, too frail?

Snug in my nest of vocabularies, safe in my view,
I've had to jump up three, four times, just to
tell Something Awful out there to be careful of you.

Phu-eet, a more and more panicky piping, *phu-eet*!
And not meaning anything I mean. In the grammar of *tweet*
why did we ever say birds should sound *sweet, sweet*?

Pity the Birds

(for Charles Elvin who said, 'Poetry should protest')

Pity
the persistent clamour of a song thrush
I can't see;
the gull's vacant wail, its sea-saw
yodel of injury;
that black and white wagtail bobbing
for a meal of midges;
rapacious Mrs Blackbird shopping on foot
in the hedges;
even yesterday's warbler, lying stiff on the step
to the barn,
olive green wings torn awry by the wind,
eyes gone,
but with tri-clawed reptilian feet still
hungrily curled.

Not one of them gened to protest
against the world.

Comet

(i.m. Lewis Lloyd, 1939–1996, Welsh historian
'who toiled at the quarry face of history')

Bad days end just like good days,
wrapping themselves with relief in simple extinction,
supper dishes washed and tidily put away,
video rewinding with a soft purr,
bedside light switched on, switched off, as we sink,
in the habit of marriage, into middle-aged sleep.
In this April for-two-steady-weeks-cloudless sky
the new comet's flight-path keeps to schedule,
hurtling mathematically *according to his circuit,*
but by us deserted in its north-west diamond patch.
Get up in the night, and the corner of your eye
catches it sooner than a searching gaze.

By morning it has set beyond belief,
portent or presence filtered lightly through
spread nets of consciousness,
received, if at all, as subliminal unease.
A beetle pulls to a halt in its trek across kitchen vinyl.
A spider out of the drain fakes *rigor mortis*
on killing fields of wet enamel.
Instinctive. Have you noticed
how a butterfly, starved, just out of its chrysalis
but struck, somehow, by a look, will cancel its programme
of fluttering visits and, locked to a petal,
transform itself into a leaf?

Lives. Terrified of shadows.
Where does time go when memory loosens its orbit
and whirls into the night?
In wild trajectories of broken light,
first this, then that dead face flares and burns out.
Where's the soul of immense Lewis, maritime historian
shadowed by his shadow, now that his blurred bulk,
slurring home at midnight, learned and drunk,
has berthed in the sound harbour of his books?
And still what in him matters is the matter of Wales.
There, blazing back of my eyelids, comets' tails,
indelible Vs grooved in salt water by wrecked prows.

The Wrekin

(a version from the Welsh of Dewi Stephen Jones)

Overnight it climbs like a snail
    to a corner of the window,
so that the sun each day
    greets a new form of the same animal.
A birth mound. A tumulus,
    neither watch tower nor turret;
more a muscle slewed to the south-east
    hiding its rounded horns.

I examine a homely shape
    slumped in its shell,
a foot stuck fast to the window pane,
    a slipper clamped in a shackle.
And when night arrives to prise it loose,
    I imagine it sliding back softly
along a wet, silvery track
    to a tunnel in the dark.

For coming and going is its nature,
    like the nature of the coming-and-going
generations who built and bred here,
    leaving raw fingerprints on the land:
    hunters, cultivators, destroyers,
    spillers of blood and seed,
brothers and enemies. Stone, bronze and iron
    precipitates of history.

An omphalos, then, a centre that to many
    was barrow and womb,
threshold for the long perished living,
    household for the ever-present dead.
So the river flows on to the sea,
    and between myself
and the ocean of air above me
    red elder berries shake in the wind.

How long has the mountain been an eye
        fixed above the human flow,
constant through continual change? MARS ULTOR
        stamped on the sestertius;
the Roman villa's buried shrine to Venus,
        traces of a tessellated floor.
Civilisation ghosts the wreck of Uricon,
        a dragon heart incarnadine with war.

Shall we say that at a turning point in history
        a Mount of Olives rose
above our plains? Is it Golgotha again
        where Heledd, in her grief,
was Mary Magdalene? How far or near
        is the mountain on the rim of the world?
What would our lowland lives be like
        without its frame?

Look out again this morning,
        it's a print on dirty canvas,
a stone bridge out of pre-history,
        coloured thickbrown; peat smoke
cresting the ridge and drifting down,
        a shape detached, displaced,
one of my own vertebrae,
        an unearthed bone.

But no, look again, see how
        the heavy lowered eyelid
of the cloud has lifted now.
        And that's the sun,
it must be sunlight striking straight
        down on the rock face,
lighting fires of pure annihilation
        like a lens.

But gifting me with insight, too,
        so I see the mountain,
the circumference of my own small life,
        consumed, extinguished
on my shore; my ocean purged of stars.
        One day I'll set my prow,
strip off my longings, cut the anchor line and go.
        See, I'm almost naked now.

Why Take Against Mythology? (1)

That twilight skyline, for example,
the more I look at it,
the more I see a skull
crushed into the hill, nose
chipped flat, jaw
thrust up, full bush of
genitals stirring just
in the right place.

See him? No, stand
here, clear of the house.
Uncork a magnum
of imagination, man!
Inflame your heart
with my enchanted giant.
Figure his resurrection
in your dreams, or art.

But make him art, not fact.
For when daylight comes back
it will tear him apart.
And how could we
live in a Wales
made of ice-cut rock? No tales
in the making of mountains,
no mind in the dark?

Why Take Against Mythology? (2)

Why, love, do you persist
in personifying natural events?
That's not imagination, it's arrogance –
locating fate in stars, off-loading
guilt on rocks! They were liquid once,
you know, eons before
our first unpurposeful cells
commenced their crawl.

You like to imagine?
Imagine nuclei moiling themselves
alive in steamy crevices,
continents travelling and clashing.
Then, three miles high, a grinding
plain of ice, a Pleistocene caul,
gouging, sculpting, furrowing
this scoop of valley.

Before art, lichens delicately
etched that cliff face.
Millions of millennia formed
bracken, heather, gorse.
Such facts are minted from imagination!
And they'll raise us above ourselves
once daft mankind
stops conjuring out of mass and force
false spirit-shadows of his own mind.

False Flowers
(for Caroline Ireland)

They were to have been a love gift,
but when she slit the paper funnel,
they both saw they were fake; false flowers
he'd picked in haste from the store's display,
handmade coloured stuff, stiff as crinoline.

Instantly she thought of women's hands
cutting in grimy light by a sweatshop window;
rough plank tables strewn with cut-out
flower heads: lily, iris, primula, scentless
chrysanthemums, pistils rigged on wire
in crowns of sponge-tipped stamens,
sepals and petals perfect, perfectly
immune to menaces from the garden.

Why so wrong, so... flattening? Why not instead
symbols of unchanging love?
$\qquad\qquad\qquad$ Yet pretty enough,
she considered, arranging them in a vase
with dry grass and last summer's hydrangeas
whose deadness was still (how to put it?)
alive, or maybe the other side of life.
Two sides, really, of the same thing?

She laughed a little, such ideas were embarrassing
even when kept to oneself,
but her train of thought
carried her in its private tunnel through supper,
and at bedtime, brushing her teeth,
she happened to look up at the moon.
Its sunlit face was turned, as always, in her direction.
The full moon, she couldn't help thinking,
though we see only half of it.

It was an insight she decided she could
share with him, but when he joined her
and together they lay in the dark,
there seemed no reason to say anything.
The words, in any case, would be wrong,
would escape or disfigure her meaning.
Good was the syllable she murmured to him,
fading into sleep. And just for a split second,
teetering on the verge of it, she believed
everything that had to be was understood.

Kosovo Surprised by Mozart
(Bernard Roberts playing K. No. 533, 11 April 1999)

Lovely chromatic Mozart, talk to me
in your language of intimate, arithmetical
progression. Perform with this performer.
Hold that diminished seventh's cutting edge
close against the dominant until it
skylarks away from the tonic's expectant
cages to a charmed high of almost
imperceptible *rallentando*, only to
circle back lightly into the right key.

Why does what is known of happiness,
like sadness, find insignia in harmony?
Your genes were a template of musical
grammar from the hour of your birth.
You must have translated straight from
sensation into sound, ignoring the tongue's
barbed wire at disputed borders. How young
you were, how unfinished your work of
spinning tempi into timelessness.

Easy it may be to bless and be blessed
in the *terra cognita* of Pythagoras, but
who lives there long? Young hungry hours can't
help but devour us, hacking from east to west
through this eleventh day, fourth month, last year
of the twentieth century. An uninhabited body is
slashed and displayed on a pole. It's not unusual
for flesh to be pummelled, pistol-whipped,
groin-kicked, machine-gunned under arrest.

For news is the news, and our cameras favour
burying sufferers alive in rewindable footage.
And your spirit? Escaped long ago in a passion
of inky dots. It's for ten live fingers to decode you –
leapfrogging over the rubble, the incurable hospital,
the wreck of the temple, the cries and imploring hands.
We accuse you, Herr Mozart, of not representing our age.
Simplified, rarefied, perfectionist as ever,
punish us in the key of F Major.

Leaving

Habits the hands have, reaching for this and that,
    (tea kettle, orange squeezer, milk jug,
    frying pan, sugar jar, coffee mug)
manipulate, or make, a habitat,
become its *genii loci*, working on
quietly in the kitchen when you've gone.

Objects a house keeps safe on hooks and shelves
    (climbing boots, garden tools, backpacks
    bird feeders, tennis balls, anoraks)
the day you leave them bleakly to themselves,
do they decide how long, behind the door,
to keep your personality in store?

Good Bishop Berkeley made the objects stay
just where we leave them when we go away
by lending them to God. If so, God's mind
is crammed with things abandoned by mankind
    (featherbeds, chamber pots, flint lighters,
    quill pens, sealing wax, typewriters),

an archive of the infinitely there.
But there for whom? For what museum? And where?
I like to think of spiders, moths, white worms
leading their natural lives in empty rooms
    (egg-sacks, mouse-litter, dead flies,
     cobwebs, silverfish, small eyes)

while my possessions cease to study me
    (*Emma, The Signet Shakespeare, Saving Whales.*
    Living with Mushrooms, Leviathan, Wild Wales).
Habit by habit, they sink through time to be
one with the mind or instinct of the place,
home in its shadowy silence and stone space.

Old Wife's Tale

'Well then, goodbye,' she said coldly,
'hot men must mate.'

But the energy of injury –
oh, it hurts like hate.

On Going Deaf

I've lost a sense. Why should I care?
Searching myself, I find a spare.
I keep that sixth sense in repair
And set it deftly, like a snare.

A Luxury

No, trilobites didn't
discuss
the future of fossils.

Pterodactyls
formed no
theology of flight.

Did Triceratops ever
lie awake
miserating all night,

or vainly believe that
pills, prayers
or a psychoanalyst

could make everything
wrong
go right?

I'm questioning
the weight
of the human cortex

and what it costs
per life
to ship its freight.

Why, among billions
of killer zooids,
do hominids alone

look in upon
themselves
and curse their fate?

It's not as if pets
and parakeets
and collared turtle-doves

(their dreamy summer
syncopated moan)
and sonic self-locating bats,

and great cetaceans,
iridescent porpoises –
or even head lice,

worms and scuttling feeders
under tombstones –
existed without purposes.

More that the creatures,
lacking our rig
of impudent imagination, miss

(besides our self-propelling genius)
our luxury
of self-destructiveness.

All might have been
explained had
vegetarian Eve before her fall

been true to God's
or Darwin's picture,
or even true at all.

When chance made us
blind chains of protein
built us to advance

by interlacing
with our hardware
something like a dance.

Two steps forward,
two steps
back, and every gain

we grab from nature
in her coin
we have to pay for.

O Time that knows no
soon or late,
be quick, when cycling through us

the cerebral mix
that makes us great
tells nature to undo us.

Burning the News

Burning last week's hot news
to kindle this cool night's fire;
burning big names from the news,
making ash of their faces and views,
ha ha, as the flames jag higher
in hungrier and hungrier desire,
I love to pretend we could choose
a more face-saving way to expire.

But burning is something we share
with the *Sun* (and the *Guardian* and *Mail*)
on a planet compounded of air
and the wonderful stuff in its care.
We've been given bit parts in a tale
that is burning us, female and male,
in a furnace of joyous despair.
No bribe to secede can prevail.

Oysters

The fat man laughed because
the restaurant told him to,
though the oysters that slipped
at atrocious expense
through his pinguid lips
were poisonous,
and the hock at his elbow
hardly less,
and the lady, too,
so svelt in the crypt
of her basilisk dress
was dangerous
beyond the laughable.
Wasn't that diamond
clipped
at her cleavage
an oyster between
white dunes on a beach,
grown luscious on sewage's
steamy tureen
of barely detectable
radioactive garbage?

All There Was

Bursting into your study,
Believing you were there,
Hi, Darling! I entrusted
To electric air.

My words crusted the silence.
No whisper tunnelled out.
A pile of learned magazines,
And open book about

Catastrophe or chaos,
A goose-lamp bent to see
Pencil-scribbled margins,
Page 202 and 3.

Monitor gently pulsing,
A half mug's sludgy brew,
Two plastic bags, a slipper –
All that was left of you.

To Witness Pain Is a Different Form of Pain

The worm in the spine.
The word on the tongue.
        Not the same.
We speak of 'pain'.
The sufferer won't suffer it
        to be tamed.

There's a shyness, no,
        a privacy,
a pride in us. Don't divide us
        into best and lesser.

Some of us, 'brave?' 'clever?'
watch at the mouth of it.
        A woman vanishes,
eyes full of it, into it,
the grey cave of pain.
        An animal drills
unspeakable growth for cover.

Outside we pace in guilt.
Ah, 'guilt', another name.

        Not to reproach
is tact she learns to suffer.
And not to relax her speechless
        grip on power.

The Theologian's Confession

Turning his last days page by page,
Man is a God-thing, Anselm murmurs,
And God a man-thing made of language.
Three in One. But I? am embers.

Booked by my bracket's final numbers,
I will be lost in the dash between
Proof that confuses and encumbers
And truth so plain it won't be seen.

Whistler's *Gentleman by the Sea*

'Nature, who for once has sung in tune,
sings her exquisite songs to the artist alone.'
J.M. WHISTLER, 1885

He knew himself as Sunday in a hat,
Patrolling borders of a century that
Lectured the waves and watched them shuffling back.

Till paint abstracted him from joy of this,
Cancelled the certainty he must exist,
And made of him a gentlemanly mist.

Where does the ocean end, the man begin?
Rain and the waves debate beneath his skin.
Tides of his pearl-grey blood drag out and in,

While, soothed and veiled, the moody water breathes
Cerulean horizontals through his knees.
Nature persuades all elements to please

When to the artist Nature sings alone.
Then Art advises Nature in its own
Linseed-on-canvas, frame-begetting tone.

III

A Parable for Norman
(i.m. Norman MacCaig)

Three vast unavoidable ladies,
Time, Fate and Boredom,
come knocking at your door.

What have you got in that school bag?
You eye Ms Time suspiciously.

A full load of years, says she
in a soothing tone.
Friendships, books, bottles,
a few stones.

And I have to buy the lot? – courtly
through your smoker's cough.

Aye, but you pay by the day, dear,
just out of what you've got.
Smiling, she unpacks an invisible file
and then, predictably, flies off.

Flexing undependable eyebrows,
Ms Fate steps up next,
snapping back the hasps
of a departmental briefcase.

What's this?
A display of bone-framed photographs,
all of your face –
half Rose Street bard
presiding graciously in bars
full of like spirits,

half man of Assynt.
Two mistresses, Suilven and Pollaidh,
loom in attendance,
surrounded by a family of
lovely little wild blue lochans.

Exactly what I ordered,
you compliment her, bowing your thanks.

But finally, the third in the trio,
shapeless and clammy with cobwebs,
yawns her way in.
A perfect host even to the nastiest,
you nod, I've been expecting you.
Sit down if you must,
but don't think you'll make yourself welcome.

Old Mrs Boredom sighs and spreads herself
stickily over furniture and pictures.
If you don't like the feel of me, Norman,
why not take up with my kids?

Such as?

Immemorial Magnificence, for a start.
Or Mystical Real Palpable Otherness.

Ugly and pleonastic, you shudder,
and *un*real into the bargain.

No? Well, there's always Venus,
she's real, you'll agree, and popular.

Toute entière à sa proie attachée?
Spare me, spare me! – as you
gravitate towards your desk
unscrewing your fountain pen.

Mars, then, glorious Mars,
on the bloody side of your imagination.
All the best poets write about him.

Not I, you say dryly.
And down go ten lines of
ultra expensive highland wit
with a bitter sting in the finish.

Looking up, you're surprised.
Your drab interlocutress is gathering her
shadows and herding them briskly
through the door. Ye'll no get
(her Parthian shot)
the slightest citation on Parnassus!

And your family (his countershot)
does not stir the slightest flutter
in my heart. Reflecting, he calls after her,
Don't you have a sister called Peace?
But she's gone. Or she just doesn't answer.

Poem for Harry Fainlight

(d. 1982)

Tree, a silence
voiced by wind.

Wind, breath
with a tree's body.

Axe the bole,
plane the boards.

Here is Art,
the polished instrument,
casket and corpse.

Dum Vixi Tacui
Mortua Dulce Cano

The harp's motto
will do for the harpist's apology.

But your poems, Harry,
those Welsh oaks
stunted by the wind's scream?

They were always
transforming your wrong life
into their live silence.

The harp's Latin motto: '*When alive I was silent.*
In death I sweetly sing.'

Invocation and Interruption
(i.m. Ted Hughes)

Gigantic iron hawk
coal-feathered like a crow,
tar-coated cave bird,
werewolf, wodwo,

you've flown away now,
where have you flown to?

was how this poem began
before the shade of a voice
fell on my hand.
I was going to invoke
a many-sided Hughes and refer
to his poems and Sylvia's;
it was to be called 'Totem'

when I felt that faint weight
of exhaled disapproval. Was it
disappointment?
No shadow from a shaman-flight,
no daemonic revelation;
just a sad discolouring of the air,
an indefinable pressure.

'Please don't imagine I have
flown anywhere,' said the silence
like a voice in deep water.
'The underworld was always a metaphor,
the life after life in which poets
are remade by their interpreters.
I'm better off here with
Sylvia and Otto, Coleridge and Ovid.
Nothing can hurt us;
we're immune to our reputations.
As for you and the others–
you'd best be getting on
with getting on.

Keep marching, keep trudging
out of the trench and stench of one century
over the wire into another.
The millennium? You're still
in the realm of blood and its thirsty ways,
so keep your head down.
Try to preserve the cave birds
at the bottom of your kit
and Prospero's magic in your hip flask.

Don't sell yourself or your poems
for a mess of verbiage. Oh, yes,
and warn those agribusiness bastards
against abusing the Goddess.
Once riled, she tends to avenge herself
without discriminating between
lovers and rapists.
Take special care of her fish.
Take special care of her thrushes.

And don't tell me who I was!

I'm the dream of a boy
who became a man and a lover
only by doing violence to violence.
I killed the fox that brought me poetry
smoking from the gun.
After that midnight encounter,
I set out for…where I am.
Death was my leader, tormentor,
wife, adversary, friend.
And still I'm, like herself,
an invention of my own imagination.
You'll find me in all my books.
So please, no more poems about me,
grateful as I am for the compliment.
I had the last word first, remember.
I'm going to keep things like this.'

A Present

(for Lee Harwood)

A grey undecided morning.
No wind.
It's cold, so get dressed quickly.
Step out into the new born air.
Look around.
It's yours, this shifting misty envelope,
a hospital to breathe in,
along with chaffinches and great tits
queueing for the wire feeder;
on the lichened wall beneath,
dunnocks make do with titbits.
Now a thrush in concentrated rushes
combs the pasture.
Those sheep-bitten daffodils
poke up, you'd say, out of nowhere,
though moles know
what's going on down there,
rebuilding under their slagheaps
a secret city.

But your secret's up in the hills,
so pull on your socks, boots, woolly hat
and layers of windproofing.
Fill up your thermos, shoulder your pack.
The ice age planed these mountains down for you
too many millennia ago to be
reasonably thanked.
They're a gift, like your life,
that never thought to be a life.
Moelfre, Rhinog Fawr, Y Llethr, Diphwys,
bald monitors bearded with cloud,
at rest in their Welsh nomenclature.

And like living things, old.
So old they're not likely to look older
when one day you don't remember them;
when lovers and readers you can't know about

get up at six or seven on chill winter mornings
to greet them, choosing, maybe,
certain words of yours to remember you.

Here's a present, the gift of a perfect view
straight back to a future that,
despite the computer, won't change in a hurry.
Shall I tell you what happened
in mid-February, 2099?
A soft cloud clung to the summit of Foel Ddu.
The next day, thickening, it crept down,
and as the wind backed to the east,
veered south, west and north-west,
hail, sleet, sunburst and snow flurry
gave pleasure to a lonely walker, cold
but happy on the high ground,
as the sun handed him a hillside,
bright as ever green moss
shone over stone in the bronze age.
The story in the marsh was a long memory
retelling itself in a shower of gold.

Sarajevo, *June 28, 1914*

Cramped under plumes of slaughtered cock,
In uniform of High Command,
Steps, to the ticking of a clock,
Unfortunate Franz Ferdinand.

Bright upright teeth that prick the ground
Are troops set out like painted toys.
The drums beat loud, the sun beats down,
The game awaits its player boys.

And now contingency meets fact.
They drive in state along the quay.
The Duchess in a picture hat
Assumes imperial dignity.

The Duke, self-conscious, feeling stout,
Stows his accoutrements of war.
A nervous youth in black pulls out
A pin, but fails to bomb their car.

What, scenting death, can an Archduke do
But prove his blood, be madly brave,
Look to the wounded, make a show,
Snapping fat fingers at the grave?

Just such a rule directs this day.
The Mayor makes his mayor's speech.
Then Duke and Duchess drive away
To luncheon they will never reach.

The Name of the Worm

(The speaker is a 90-year-old Jewish doctor who is dying of cancer.
His niece has brought him some roses.)

Oh, hallo, good of you to come. Sorry I can't get up.
You'll find the sherry on the sideboard. I regret
that in my present condition... My dear, how thoughtful.
From your garden? Proper roses, lots of petals,
lots of prickles. *Aber süss*, that sentimental military scent –
speaking as an unsentimental, practically defunct medic.

You know, I never did understand, as a young man,
why poets made so much of roses – roses and women –
till Margaret and I were on holiday in the Austrian Alps.
August 1933. We were engaged but not yet married, since
I had my residency still to do at Bart's. I remember,
yes, a wild, spectacular place south of Brenner.
Fischleinboden. That was the inn. We were happy to be
the only English. Everyone else spoke German, very friendly.
Well, one day, three young men... no, two fit-looking chaps
and a grim official – portfolio stuffed with maps –
moved into our annex. We'd preferred it to the main chalet
as cheaper and more private. It annoyed us, the way
these newcomers assumed we'd want to drink and talk at night,
then in the daytime share their walks. Still, we were polite.
Soon it emerged that they were Nazis, only too
chuffed to meet English youth. *We would be friends with you*,
said the handsome one who spoke English. Turned out he'd been
to Cambridge, worked as a teacher in Berlin.
Passionately in love with English literature,
kept quoting from Shakespeare, knew a bit of Chaucer...
And to prove it one morning, presented Margaret with a rose.
Now Margaret, fair-skinned with auburn hair, was in those
days lovely, but her politics were redder than her hair:
Oh rose thou art sick, and the name of the worm is Hitler
– quick as a flash, making a deep, departing bow –
leaving speechless, still holding his rose, the German who,
drained to the colour of his lederhosen, stared at me.
It was the first time, I think, he'd really looked at me.
Through my thick-lensed glasses, I looked back at him.

White curtains fluttered over the Vinschgau, the sun poured in.
I broke the silence. *Excuse me*, I said, and started after her.
I watched his lips tighten, relax, smile and kiss his rose.
Next time, he said, *when you visit here, it will all be ours.*
Then in bewilderment, *Do you not also long to be a soldier?*

The Miracle of Camp 60

(The speaker is a fictive Italian ex-POW revisiting the Italian Chapel on the Orkney island of Lamb Holm in 1992.)

Amici d'arti, amici dei fiori, amici d'amore,
When in our towns they told us *go fight for Il Duce*
we Dolomiti had to go. We were…coscritti, we
had no choice. I wept when I departed from Trento,
my poor mother, my so sad new young wife.
Credi in Dio, we embraced each other as the train
stretched us apart. But then in the deeps of misery
I had some luck. My seat-partner, how do you say,
was Chiocchetti. L'artista Domenico Chiocchetti
of Moena, a man very sensitive…you understand?
And so he saw my tears. With him he kept always –
like this, around his neck – a spiritual picture,
Madonna delle Olive – Our Lady of the Olives,
of our great Italian painter, Nicolo Barabina.
This medallion Domenico let me hold, for hope,
as the train transported us human meats to Roma,
then to Tunis, to Egitto, to fight the war.
See over the altar, the Madonna of Chiocchetti,
Regina Pacis, Ora Pro Nobis. As we prayed many many times
in that desert of death under the stars.
Our prayers were answered when you Britons beat us.
No more did we have to fear the brute Tedeschi.
So we were glad. Not to be prisoners, you understand,
but to be not any longer soldiers, while we were sad
not to go home. We did not know what was happening
in our country, to our families. When we came to Orkney,
we did not know where we were, so far, so… smorta,
this terrible island, not one tree, not one flower.
Only polvere, calcina, cemento…everywhere
filo barbato, all sunshine strangled in it, and huts
we would use for pigs in Italy, to share.

Only Chiocchetti saw… a holy place.
Look, he pointed through the wires, the azure water,
isole, islands, emerald in the sea. He was painting them
already in his head while we worked through rain and wind
to build the barriers. Labour we did not mind.

Better to work than to despair. Even so,
there was too much time to think of home.
Before the war my occupation was giardinere.
I made gardens for the city of Merano.
After I went back, I was the capo. One day on Lamb Holm
I spied among the rocks a small flower, an iris rare
in Italy, and to myself I said, here we could grow piante,
make little beds, walkways, sentieri.

So with some men I went to the Commandante.
Please may we have some seeds. Seeds? He was surprised.
He found us seeds and bulbs, in some months we had iris,
geranio, calendula, lupini, giglio – you say lily?
We made your desert bloom. Now, why not a piazza with a statue?
OK, says Chiocchetti, without marble I carve cemento;
without bronze, I twist barbed wire. Eccola!
The marvel he created. San Giorgio spearing the dragon.
To show the wish of us Italians to exterminate evil.
Into the base we put our names and coins we saved
from home. Our padre, Gioachino Giacobazzi, swung his censer.
We wept for sadness and joy because from memory
we had made in our ugly camp a dream of Italy.

Allora, came winter and the long nights. We found
some space for a teatro. Talented men among us played
harmonica, mandolin. Always we prisoners had the spirit
to make beauty, but up to that time we had no church,
no place of God to celebrate mass. Yet once again
Il padre, Chiocchetti and myself were called to Major Buckland,
'Signori, you are Catholic. Do you not need a chapel?'
That English Major was, I think, exceptional. Under his
traditional reserve beat surely the Italian heart.
A short time and two new huts appeared, placed end to end,
like so – to make one bigger hut.
And now the talent of Chiocchetti became genius.
He picked skilled helpers and they, too, caught fire.
Palumbo, who studied metal-working in America, contrived
from scrap – gracile, delicato – the screen of iron.
And Bruttapasta whose speciality was concrete.
Regard his altar, made out of just cemento. The same for
la facciata, colonne, campanile, pinnacoli, vetri –
painted in all colori, l'arco, i pedimenti. Also, in red stone
la testa di Cristo crocefisso that was moulded by Pinesi.

It was as if, on this far island, by the mercy of God,
we few had been chosen to prepare in a world destroyed
a home for the immortal dove who alone brings peace
to men and women. Regard – on the vault of the sanctuary
in the fresco of Chiocchetti – a dove with angels.

Mi scusate. Excuse me. I am incapable of beholding this place
without tears. War was good to us. We were prisoners
but we were happy, making our chapel beautiful.
Happier than ever again. When the war finished
we had to depart. I sobbed because we had not finished.
I wept again in Merano. La mia madre, morta…my poor wife.
You know what i bruti soldati did to beautiful women.
We could not have children. To forgive myself for joy
while my loved ones suffered – so many suffered –
it was not easy. Chiocchetti did not come home with us.
He stayed to complete his font, and when I met him in Moena –
many many years later – he told me he, too, felt guilty.
But guilt is not right, he said, for art is joy.
Short is our suffering in this life, joy is forever.

Now an old man, I visit again our joyful chapel
to read in your language a prayer of blessed Francis.

Lord, make me an instrument of peace.
Where there is hatred, let me sow love,
where there is injury, pardon,
where there is darkness, light,
where there is sadness…gioia, la gioia.

A Ballad for Apothecaries

Being a Poem to Honour the Memory of
Nicholas Culpeper, Gent.
Puritan, Apothecary, Herbalist, Astologer
Who in the year of our Lord 1649
Did publish *A PHYSICAL DIRECTORY*
A translation from the Latin of the London Despensatory
made by the College of Physicians
'Being that Book by which all Apothecaries are strictly
commanded to make all their Physicke.'

In sixteen-hundred-and-sixteen
(The year Will Shakespeare died),
Earth made a pact with a curious star,
And a newborn baby cried.

Queen Bess's bright spring was over,
James Stuart frowned from the throne;
A more turbulent, seditious people
England had never known.

Now, Nick was a winsome baby,
And Nick was a lively lad,
So they gowned him and sent him to Cambridge
Where he went, said the priests, to the bad.

For though he excelled in Latin
And could rattle the Gospels in Greek,
He thought to himself, there's more to be said
Than the ancients knew how to speak.

He was led to alchemical studies
Through a deep Paracelsian text.
He took up the art of astrology first,
And the science of botany next.

To the theories of Galen he listened,
And to those of Hippocrates, too,
But he said to himself, there's more to be done
Than the ancients knew how to do.

For though Dr Tradition's a rich man,
He charges a rich man's fee.
Dr Reason and Dr Experience
Are my guides in philosophy.

The College of Learned Physicians
Prescribes for the ruling class:
Physick for the ills of the great, they sneer,
Won't do for the vulgar mass.

But I say the heart of a beggar
Is as true as the heart of a king,
And the English blood in our English veins
Is of equal valuing.

Poor Nick fell in love with an heiress,
But en route to their desperate tryst,
The lady was struck down by lightning
Before they'd embrased or kissed.

So our hero consulted the Heavens
Where he saw he was fated to be
A friend to the sick and the humble
But the Great World's enemy.

Nick packed up his books in Cambridge
And came down without a degree
To inspirit Red Lion Street, Spitalfields,
With his fiery humanity.

As a reckless, unlicensed physician,
He was moved to disseminate
Cures for the ills of the body
With cures for the ills of the state.

Who knows what horrors would have happened
To Nicholas Culpeper, Gent.,
If the king hadn't driven his kingdom
Into war with Parliament.

In the ranks of the New Model Army
Nick fought with the medical men,
Till a Royalist bullet at Newbury
Shot him back to his thundering pen.

'Scholars are the people's jailors,
And Latin's their jail, ' he roared,
'Our fates are in thrall to knowledge;
Vile men would have knowledge obscured!'

When they toppled King Charles's head off
Nick Culpeper cried, 'Amen!'
It's well that he died before the day
They stuck it on again.

Still, English tongues won their freedom
In those turbulent years set apart;
And the wise, they cherish Nick's courage
While they cheer his compassionate heart.

So whenever you stop in a chemist's
For an aspirin or salve for a sore,
Give a thought to Nicholas Culpeper
Who dispensed to the London poor.

For cures for the ills of the body
Are cures for the ills of the mind;
And a welfare state is a sick state
When the dumb are led by the blind.

NOTE: In a series of prefaces to this best-selling manual in English
(reprinted at least fourteen times before 1718) Culpeper denounced
the College of Physicians who secured their monopoly by keeping
the secrets of medicine in the Latin language – just as Rome's
priests, before the Reformation, had maintained power by preserving

the mysteries of the Bible in Latin. Culpeper's translation, he declared, was made 'out of pure pity to the commonality of England... many of whom to my knowledge have perished either for want of money to fee a physician or want of knowledge of a remedy happily growing in their garden.'

When the victory of the Parliamentarian Army was still in doubt, Culpeper was branded by the Royalist *Mecurious Pragmaticus* as an Anabaptist 'who had arrived at the battlement of an Absolute Atheist, and by two years drunken labour hath Gallimawfred the apothecaries book into nonsense, mixing every receipt therein with some scruples at least of rebellion or atheism, besides the danger of poisoning men's bodies. And (to supply his drunkenness and lechery with a thirty-shilling award) endeavoured to bring into obloquy the famous Societies of Apothecaries and Chyrugeons.' Such abuses, all of them unfounded, were levelled by his political opponents. Even during the Cromwellian interregnum, a broadside appeared (1652) entitled 'A farm in Spittlefields where all the knick-knacks of astrology are exposed to open sale, where Nicholas Culpeper brings under his velvet jacket: 1. His chalinges against the Doctors of Physick, 2. A Pocket Medicine. 3. An Abnormal Circle.'

Culpeper's *London Dispensary*, however, together with a *Directory for Midwives* and others of his 79 books and pamphlets, continued to sell in large numbers. In 1652-3, he brought out his celebrated herbal under the title of *The English Physitian: or, an Astrological-Physical Discourse of the Vulgar Herbs of this Nation, Being a Compleat Method of Physick, whereby a man may preserve his Body in Health, or cure himself, being sick, for three pence charge, with such things as grow in England, they being most fit for English Bodies.*

Though Culpeper may have been in some ways a charlatan, his *Dispensary* remained in print into the 18th century and his *English Physitian* continues to be the most celebrated of English herbals even today. Sadly, Culpeper's remedies, praised and prized by the London poor, were not able to prevent his death at 38 (from an old wound received while he was fighting in the Parliamentarian Army) nor the deaths of six of his seven children who predeceased him.

Postscriptum

Now I am dead,
no words,
just a wine
of my choosing.

Drink to my
mute consent,
my rite of
dissolving.

Over my chalk
eyelids and wax skin
let a wild
reticence in.

Not a tear
or false look.
Poems, stay there
in your book.

Should passion
attend me,
let it flow freely
through Messiaen's

End of Time Quartet:
unendurable riddles
for the clarinet,
resolved in a fiddle's

remorseless,
forgiving ascent.

Anne Stevenson, born in England of American parents, grew up in the States but has lived in Britain for most of her adult life. She has published twelve collections of poetry, a book of essays, *Between the Iceberg and the Ship* (1998), a recent critical study, *Five Looks at Elizabeth Bishop* (1998), and a biography of Sylvia Plath, *Bitter Fame* (1989).

Granny Scarecrow is her first collection since *The Collected Poems 1955-1995* (now available from Bloodaxe) was published by Oxford University Press in 1996. She reads poems from these two books on *The Poetry Quartets 6* (The British Council/Bloodaxe Books, 2000), a double-cassette shared with Moniza Alvi, Michael Donaghy and George Szirtes.